Coco-Nutty Peach Smoothie

2 peaches, stoned
225ml/8floz/1 cup canned coconut milk
½ tsp almond essence (extract)
50g/2oz/½ cup ratafia biscuits (almond-
flavoured dried macaroons, similar to
Amaretti biscuits), broken into pieces

1 Place the peaches, coconut milk, almond essence (extract), and half the biscuits in a blender; blend until smooth.

2 Pour into glasses and chill well.

3 Sprinkle the remaining biscuits on top just before serving.

Apricot, Almond, and Coconut Smoothie: Replace the peaches with 12 stoned apricots.

Nectarine, Almond, and Coconut Smoothie: Use nectarines instead of the peaches.

Mango, Almond, and Coconut Smoothie: Use 1 peeled and stoned mango instead of the peaches.

Ginger Cream Smoothie

2.5cm/1 inch piece of ginger root,
peeled and grated
1 tbsp clear honey
125ml/4floz/½ cup natural (plain) yogurt
2 scoops vanilla ice cream

1 Place the ginger, honey, yogurt, and ice cream in a blender; blend until smooth.

2 Serve immediately.

Choc 'n' Ginger Cream Smoothie: Use 2 scoops of chocolate ice cream in place of the vanilla ice cream.

Toffee 'n' Ginger Smoothie: Use toffee-flavoured yogurt and toffee or vanilla ice cream.

for a berry merry life

Strawberry Jam Shake

115g/4oz/1 cup strawberries, washed
   and hulled
2 tbsp strawberry jam
4 scoops strawberry ice cream
300ml/10floz/1¼ cups cold milk

1 Place the strawberries, jam, and two scoops of ice cream in a blender and blend until smooth.

2 With the machine running, gradually pour in the milk and blend until frothy.

3 Place a scoop of ice cream into each of two glasses and pour the milk shake over the ice cream.

Raspberry Jam Shake: Use fresh or frozen raspberries, raspberry jam, and raspberry ripple ice cream instead of the strawberry options.

Apricot Jam Shake: Use fresh apricots, apricot jam, and vanilla ice cream instead of the strawberry options.

Tiramisu Smoothie

225g/8oz/1 cup mascarpone cheese
2–3 tbsp icing (confectioners') sugar
225ml/8oz/1 cup cold coffee
A little grated chocolate
Sponge fingers to serve

1 Place the mascarpone cheese, sugar, and coffee in a blender and blend until smooth, or whisk together in a bowl.

2 Pour into glasses and sprinkle a little grated chocolate on top.

3 Serve with the sponge fingers.

Warm Tiramisu Smoothie: Use hot coffee for a warm smoothie.

Papaya and Coconut Cream

½ papaya, peeled, seeded, and cut
  into chunks
6–8 tbsp coconut milk
Juice of 1 lime

1 Place the papaya in a blender and
  add the coconut milk and lime juice.

2 Blend until smooth. If too thick, add
  a little extra coconut milk or water.

3 Pour into glasses to serve.

Mango and Coconut Cream: Replace
the papaya with mango.

Spicy Coconut Cream: Replace the
papaya with 2 peeled bananas and add
1 tsp mixed spice (allspice).

Iced Mocha Smoothie

2 tbsp cocoa powder
1 tbsp instant coffee granules
1 tbsp muscovado sugar (dark
  brown sugar)
350ml/12floz/1½ cups milk
4 tbsp single (light) or double (heavy)
  cream

1 Place the cocoa powder, coffee granules,
  and sugar in a small heatproof bowl and
  add about 4 tbsp boiling water. Stir until
  the ingredients have dissolved.

2 Stir in the milk. Pour into a shallow
  freezer container and freeze for about
  2–4 hours until slushy.

3 Scoop into a blender, add the cream,
  and blend to break up the ice crystals.
  Serve immediately.

Iced Chocolate Smoothie: Omit the
coffee and stir the dissolved cocoa
powder and sugar into 50g/2oz melted
chocolate. Gradually whisk in the cold
milk and complete as above.

Pineapple Colada Smoothie

½ small pineapple, peeled and cut into chunks
125ml/4floz/½ cup coconut milk

1 Reserve 1 or 2 pieces of pineapple to decorate. Place the ingredients in a blender and blend until smooth.

2 Pour into glasses and decorate with reserved pineapple.

Pina Colada: Add a splash of rum and some crushed ice for a pina colada.

Mango Colada Smoothie: Add the flesh of ½ mango.

Roo-Berry and Strawberry Smoothie

250g/9oz rhubarb, cut into 2.5cm/1 inch lengths
4 tbsp caster (superfine) sugar
115g/4oz/1 cup strawberries, washed and hulled
225ml/8floz/1 cup natural (plain) yogurt

1 Place the rhubarb, sugar, and 4 tbsp of water in a small pan and cook gently for 10 minutes until softened.

2 Stir in the strawberries and remove from the heat. Let cool.

3 Place in a blender with the yogurt and blend until smooth.

4 Serve poured over ice.

Rhubarb and Raspberry Smoothie: Use raspberries instead of strawberries.

Banana Wind-Down Smoothie

Seeds of two cardamom pods
1 banana, peeled
225ml/8floz/1 cup freshly squeezed
   orange juice

1 Crush the cardamom seeds with a pestle and mortar; place in a blender.

2 Add the banana and orange juice, and blend until smooth.

3 Pour into a glass and serve.

Pineapple Wind-Down Smoothie: Use a wedge of trimmed pineapple instead of the banana.

Chamomile is known for its
restful, soothing
qualities, and it also has anti-inflammatory and antispasmodic properties that can help to settle digestive problems.

Chamomile, Orange, and Elderflower Soother

1 chamomile teabag
1 orange
1 tbsp elderflower cordial

1 Place the teabag in a heatproof jug and cover with 225ml/8floz/1 cup of boiling water; let steep for 10 minutes.

2 Remove the teabag and discard.

3 Squeeze the juice from the orange and add to the tea. Add the elderflower cordial and stir.

4 Pour into a glass and serve immediately.

Chamomile, Orange, and Blackcurrant Soother: Use a blackcurrant cordial in place of the elderflower cordial.

get peeled and feel great

Grape Slumber Juice

225g/8oz/1 cup red or green grapes
2 oranges, peeled and segmented
1 tsp lemon juice

1 Feed the grapes through a juicer, followed by the orange segments.

2 Stir in the lemon juice and serve.

Brandied Grape and Orange Juice:
Add 2 tbsp brandy to the juice.

Oat-So-Sleepy Banana Smoothie

1 tbsp fine oatmeal
225ml/8floz/1 cup milk
50g/2oz/¼ cup seedless raisins
1 small ripe banana, peeled
1 tsp clear honey

1 Place the oatmeal in small pan with the milk and bring almost to the boil, stirring occasionally.

2 Carefully pour into a blender, add the remaining ingredients, and blend until the mixture is smooth.

3 Pour into a heatproof glass or mug and serve.

Dairy-Free Oat-So-Sleepy Smoothie:
Replace the milk with soy milk.

Milk contains tryptophan, an essential amino acid that is a natural sleep inducer. If a skin forms over the milk, don't throw it away. Add it to the blender – the skin contains valuable nutrients.

Yogurt is full of **calcium** for healthy bones. Seeds add valuable good fats.

Honey Yogurt Flip

225ml/8floz/1 cup low-fat natural (plain) yogurt

2 tbsp clear honey

1 tbsp toasted mixed seeds such as pumpkin, sesame, and sunflower seeds

Ground cinnamon

1 Place the yogurt, honey, and half the seeds in a blender and blend briefly.

2 Pour into a glass and top with the remaining seeds. Sprinkle with cinnamon and serve.

Apple Honey Yogurt Flip: Add 1 peeled and cored apple to the blender.

Banana Honey Yogurt Flip: Add 1 small peeled banana to the blender.

Celery is known to have a calming restful effect and this juice should help to **promote sleep.**

Carrot and Celery Calmer

6 sticks celery, trimmed
4 carrots, trimmed
Carrot and celery sticks to serve

1 Feed the celery and carrots through a juicer and pour into glasses.

2 Serve with carrot and celery sticks.

Apple and Celery Calmer: Use 2 apples in place of the carrots.

Melon, Apple, and Raspberry Smoothie

¼ wedge galia or honeydew melon,
   peeled
2 apples, quartered
115g/4oz/¾ cup raspberries

1 Feed the melon and apples through a juicer, then pour into a blender.

2 Add the raspberries and blend to combine.

3 Pour into a glass and serve.

Melon, Apple, and Strawberry Smoothie: Use strawberries in place of the raspberries.

make my heart beat happily

Plummy Apple Juice

8 ripe plums, stoned
2 apples, quartered

1 Feed the plums and apples through a juicer.

2 Pour into a glass and serve.

Plum, Apple, and Ginger Juice: Feed a 2.5cm/1 inch piece of peeled ginger root through the juicer after the plums.

Apricot and Apple Juice: Instead of plum use apricots. Add a 2.5cm/1 inch piece of peeled ginger root if desired.

Strawberry Ripple Smoothie

150g/5oz/1¼ cups strawberries, hulled
2 scoops vanilla ice cream
½ tsp vanilla essence (extract)
225ml/8floz/1 cup milk
50g/2oz meringue nests (or cookies),
   broken into small bite-size pieces

1 Place the strawberries in a blender with 2 tbsp water and blend to a purée, pour into a small bowl, and set aside.

2 Rinse out the blender. Place the ice cream, vanilla essence (extract), milk, and half the meringue nests in the blender and blend until smooth.

3 Pour alternate layers of strawberry purée, ice cream mixture, and meringue into the glasses. Finish with a few pieces of meringue on top.

Yogurt and Meringue Smoothie: Use vanilla yogurt in place of the ice cream.

Raspberry Ripple Smoothie: Use raspberries instead of strawberries.

Apple Custard Crumble

2 apples, peeled, cored, and sliced
225ml/8floz/1 cup ready-made custard
   (store-bought custard vanilla pudding)
125ml/4floz/½ cup milk
1 small granola bar, crumbled

1 Place the apples in a small pan with 4 tbsp water and cook over a low heat until soft. Allow to cool completely.

2 Spoon into a blender and add the custard, milk, and half the granola bar. Blend until well combined.

3 Pour into glasses and top with the remaining granola bar.

Rhubarb Custard Crumble: Replace the apples with 175g/6oz/¾ cup rhubarb cut into short lengths.

Blackberry and Apple Custard Crumble: Add 50g/2oz/⅓ cup blackberries to the blender.

This is a fabulous low-cal drink that can be enjoyed any time of the day.

Watermelon and Ginger Refresher

450g/1lb/3 cups watermelon, peeled and cut into chunks
1cm/½ inch piece of ginger root, peeled
A little lemon juice
Sugar to taste

1 Feed the watermelon, followed by the ginger, through a juicer. Or blend in a blender, but grate the ginger first.

2 Pour into glasses and stir in a little lemon juice. Sweeten with a little sugar if required.

Melon and Ginger Refresher: Use a different variety of melon such as galia or honeydew melon.

Celery and Rocket Lift

2 sticks celery
Handful of rocket (arugula) leaves
225g/8oz/1 cup green grapes
Celery sticks to serve

1 Feed the ingredients through a juicer in the order listed.

2 Pour over crushed ice and add the celery sticks to stir.

Snappy Celery and Rocket Lift:
Add a few sugar snap pea pods after the grapes.

This is a great detox juice. The Klamath has protein and minerals that will give your body a boost.

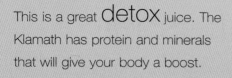

Cool Customer

4 apples, quartered
2 carrots, trimmed
1 stick celery
½ cucumber, peeled
1 tsp Klamath blue green algae
   (optional)
Cucumber slices to serve

1 Feed all the vegetables through a juicer and stir in the Klamath algae.

2 Pour over ice, decorate with cucumber slices, and serve.

Fruit and Cool: Replace the carrots with 2 pears for a fruity detox juice.

Pineapple Ginger Calmer

¼ pineapple, peeled
2.5cm/1 inch piece of ginger root, peeled
1 tbsp clear honey
Seeds of 4 cardamom pods, crushed
Strips of ginger stem or pinch of grated
    nutmeg to serve

1 Place all the ingredients in a blender
with 125ml/4 floz/½ cup of water. Blend
until smooth.

2 Thin the smoothie down to a desired
consistency with more water. If you have
an upset stomach, dilute the smoothie
and drink slowly.

3 Pour into a glass and decorate with the
strips of stem ginger or sprinkle with
nutmeg if desired.

Papaya Ginger Calmer: Use 1 papaya
in place of the pineapple.

For an **upset stomach,**
this drink contains pineapple,
which can help the digestive tract,
ginger, and cardamom, which can
relieve vomiting.

Minty Tummy Calmer

225g/8oz/2 cups strawberries, hulled
1 lime
2 tbsp freshly chopped mint
1–2 tbsp clear honey or maple syrup
(optional)

1 Feed the strawberries through a juicer.

2 Squeeze the juice from the lime and stir into the strawberry juice.

3 Stir in the chopped mint. Sweeten with a little honey or maple syrup if desired.

4 Pour into a glass and serve.

Strawberry Tummy Calmer: Add the juice of 1 lemon instead of lime.

Strawberry and Black Pepper Juice

350g/12oz /1½ cups strawberries, washed and hulled
2 apples, quartered
¼ tsp crushed black pepper

1 Feed the strawberries and apples through a juicer.

2 Stir in the pepper and serve.

Strawberry and Balsamic Juice: Add ½ tsp balsamic vinegar with the pepper for a fabulous tang.

Strawberries contain the phytochemical ellagic acid, which is believed to help prevent cancer, making this sweet juice a healthy choice.

Fennel and carrot juice creates a popular combination that has been used for centuries as a traditional remedy for poor eyesight. This combination is also used to help relieve headaches and may help menopausal or menstrual problems too.

Bright-Eyed Woman

1 fennel bulb, trimmed
3 carrots, trimmed

1 Feed the fennel and carrots through a juicer.

2 Pour into a glass and add ice if required.

Sprouty Bright-Eyed Woman: Add a handful of alfalfa sprouts, which are high in vitamins A, C, and K.

Green Bright-Eyed Woman: Add 1 carrot and ½ an avocado – it is high in vitamin E, which is good for healthy skin.

Berry Booster

Three or four 85g/3oz/¾ cup portions of: strawberries, blackberries, raspberries, blueberries, loganberries, bilberries, or cherries, pitted
A little clear honey (optional)

1 Feed the berries of your choice through a juicer.

2 Sweeten with a little honey if desired.

Berry and Orange Booster: Substitute one portion of berries with 125ml/4floz/½ cup fresh orange juice.

pack a healthy punch

Carrot, Parsnip, and Avocado Blemish Blaster

2 large carrots, trimmed
1 parsnip, trimmed and cut into chunks
1 avocado, peeled and stoned
½ lemon

1 Feed the carrots and parsnips through a juicer.

2 Place the avocado in a blender, then add the carrot, parsnip, and lemon juices. Blend until smooth.

3 Pour into a glass and serve.

Carrot, Apple, and Avocado Smoothie: Use 2 carrots, 1 apple, and the avocado.

This is a good healing juice for people with acne or other skin complaints. The smoothie is high in vitamin E, which is important for healthy skin.

Apple and melons are both great for **detoxing** the body.

Melon, Blackberry, and Apple Detox

¼ wedge galia or honeydew melon, peeled

115g/4oz/1 cup blackberries, washed and hulled

175ml/6 floz/¾ cup apple juice

1 Place the melon and blackberries in a blender with the apple juice and blend until smooth.

2 Pour over ice if desired and serve.

Melon, Raspberry, and Apple Smoothie: Replace the blackberries with raspberries for a lighter smoothie.

Bloody Mary

8 large ripe tomatoes, quartered
4 spring onions (scallions), trimmed
Dash Tabasco sauce
Dash Worcestershire sauce
1 tsp lemon juice
3 tbsp vodka
4 sticks celery to serve

1 Feed the tomatoes and onions through a juicer.

2 Stir in the Tabasco and Worcestershire sauces and lemon juice.

3 Stir in the vodka and serve over ice with a pair of celery sticks in each glass.

Note: Sprinkle a few mixed seeds over the drink for extra nutritional benefits.

Juicy Fruits

125ml/4floz/½ cup freshly squeezed orange juice
125ml/4floz/½ cup freshly pulped pineapple juice
4 tbsp tequila
75ml/3floz/⅓ cup lemon-flavored yogurt

1 Place all the ingredients in a blender and blend until smooth.

2 Pour into two tall glasses and serve.

Packed with antioxidants

Klamath blue green algae is full of nutrients that help to renourish the body if you have a drink or two too many. This drink is also packed with vitamin C, which helps the body to process alcohol faster. This is helpful for women, as the female body processes alcohol more slowly than the male body.

Wake Up

4 blood oranges
1 tsp Klamath blue green algae
12 medium strawberries, washed
   and hulled

1 Squeeze the juice from the oranges and place the juice and remaining ingredients in a blender.

2 Blend until smooth.

3 Pour over ice in glasses and serve.

Grapefruit Wake Up: Use 3 ruby grapefruit instead of the blood oranges.

Margarita

3 limes
Salt
4 tbsp tequila
2 tbsp triple sec or cointreau

1 Squeeze the juice from the limes with a citrus juicer or peel and feed through a juicer.

2 Dip the rim of two cocktail glasses into the lime juice, shaking the excess away, then dip them into salt.

3 Place the juice, tequila, and triple sec or cointreau in a blender or cocktail shaker and blend until well combined.

4 Pour into glasses and serve.

Frozen Margarita: Mix as above, then pour into a shallow container and freeze. To serve, scoop into a blender and whiz briefly.

Juicy Joints

½ mango, peeled and stoned
1 banana, peeled
1 apple, quartered
1 pear, quartered
225g/8oz/2 cups strawberries, washed
   and hulled
2 tsp tahini

1 Reserve a strawberry and a couple of slices of banana. Feed the remaining fruit through a juicer.

2 Dilute the tahini with a little hot water if required and stir into the juice.

3 Pour into glasses and decorate with reserved fruit.

Juicy Blueberry: Replace the strawberries with blueberries.

This vitamin-packed drink will help keep your muscles going through the day. Mangoes are a rich source of beta carotene, potassium, and iron. They are also high in pectin, a fibre that can help to control blood cholesterol.

Muscle Magic

1 banana, peeled
½ papaya, peeled and seeded
115g/4oz/½ cup silken tofu
225ml/8floz/1 cup whole-milk natural
   (plain) yogurt
1 tsp wheat germ
Slices papaya to serve

1 Place all the ingredients, except the
   slices of papaya, in a blender and blend
   to combine.

2 Pour into glasses, decorate with the
   papaya slices, and serve immediately.

Dairy-Free Muscle Magic: Use a soy
yogurt instead of a dairy yogurt.

Making Simple Juices

Some recipes for smoothies require the addition of fruit juices. You can use shop-bought juices, but if you have a juicer, you may want to make your own fresh juice for your smoothies, or you may simply want to make single fruit juices to drink. Here is a guide to how much juice you will get from the most popular fruit and vegetables.

To make 225ml/8floz/1 cup you will need:

Apple Juice: 4–5 apples
Orange Juice: 3–4 oranges
Pineapple Juice: ½ medium --pineapple
Tomato Juice: 4–6 medium tomatoes
Carrot Juice: 5–6 large carrots
Grapefruit Juice: 2 grapefruit
Grape Juice: 225–300g/8–10oz/
  2–2½ cups grapes
Mango Juice: 1½–2 mangoes
Pear Juice: 4–5 pears
Cherry Juice: 450–500g/1lb–1lb2oz/
  2–2½ cups cherries
Pomegranate Juice: 4–5 pomegranates

Use these quantities only as a guide. These juices were made using a centrifugal juicer (see pages 16–17). If you use a masticating juicer, you will get a larger quantity of juice because these machines are more efficient. Also remember that the amount of juice will vary between the different varieties of the same fruit and even from season to season. Ripe local fruits in season are usually juicier than fruits that have been picked unripe and flown across the world.

Juices Hints and Tips

Recipes make one to two glasses, depending on the size of your glass and the amount you want to drink. In general, vegetable juices are drunk in smaller quantities than fruit juices.

Stick to one type of measuring system. Never switch between them. Cup measurements are for standard American cups.

Always use fruit and vegetables that are in peak condition.

Wash fruit and vegetables well before use.

Prepare fruit and vegetables just before you need them. Some vitamins will start to be destroyed when you cut into the produce, and some fruit and vegetables discolor quickly.

Use organic ingredients if you want to avoid pesticide residues.

Cut vegetables into pieces that can be fed through the juicer's feeding tube easily. This will vary from machine to machine. Some machines will take whole apples, others will need the fruit or vegetables to be cut up in small pieces.

Insert soft fruit such as strawberries and blueberries slowly to extract the most juice. Follow soft fruit and leaves with a harder fruit such as an apple or a vegetable.

If you do need to store the juice, keep it in the refrigerator and add a few drops of lemon juice. (This will keep it from discoloring.)

Serve well chilled – use chilled vegetables and fruit or serve over ice.

Dilute juices for children with an equal quantity of water. You can use sparkling mineral water to create a fizzy fruit drink.

Fruit is high in fructose, a natural sugar, so people with diabetes should not drink too much. Dilute with water if necessary.

Do not drink more than 3 glasses of juice a day unless you are used to it – too much juice can cause an upset stomach.

Very dark vegetables such as beetroot (beet) and broccoli can have strong flavors. Dilute with water or with a milder flavored juice such as apple or celery if you want.

Smoothie Bases

Many smoothies are 100 percent fruit, but to blend efficiently a liquid is often added.

Fruit juice:

In 100 percent fruit smoothies, fruit juice is added if necessary. If you have a juicer, juice your own fruit to maximize the vitamin content (see pages 12–13). For speed or convenience, you can use shop-brought juices. Chilled juices not made from concentrate have the best flavor.

Yogurt:

When yogurt is added as a base it adds valuable calcium to the smoothie. Using a yogurt with live bacteria is good for the digestion, providing healthy bacteria. Greek-style yogurt will give the creamiest results but has the highest calorie content. Whole-milk yogurt can be used as a substitute for Greek-style yogurt. It adds more creaminess to the drink than a low-fat yogurt, with a calorie content that is higher than low-fat yogurt but not as high as Greek-style yogurt. Fruit-flavored yogurt may have a lot of added sugar.

Milk:

Like yogurt, milk added to smoothies provides a good source of calcium. Calcium is important for growing children, and smoothies are a good way of including milk in a fussy child's diet. Whole-fat milk has the most flavor, but for those wishing to reduce fat content, skimmed or semi-skimmed milk is better.

Cream:

For special occasions, adding single (light) or double (heavy) cream to a smoothie will give it a richer flavor.

Crème fraîche, fromage frais, quark, cottage cheese, mascarpone:

These dairy products can be added to smoothies to provide calcium and as thickeners. The fat content varies and those with a high-fat content such as full-fat crème fraîche and mascarpone should be used in moderation. Low-fat crème fraîche, cottage cheese, and fromage frais can be used more frequently. Cottage cheese and other low-fat cheeses also add protein and make a smoothie more filling. They are good additions when a smoothie is being served in place of a full meal.

Ice Cream and sorbet:

These can be added to smoothies for extra creaminess or flavor, as well as to cool the drink. They can be blended with the fruit or added by the scoop in place of ice.

Dairy substitutes:

Tofu is high in protein and low in fat. It is a good source of calcium and contains vitamin E. It has little flavor but will give your drink a more satisfying thickness and creamy texture.

Soy milk and soy yogurt can also be used as an alternative to dairy products, as can rice milk and oat milk. You can also use coconut milk, banana, and avocado to give smoothies a creamy texture and good flavor.

Smoothie Hints and Tips

Recipes make one to two glasses, depending on the size of your glass and the amount you want to drink.

Stick to one type of measuring system. Never switch between them. Cup measurements are for standard American cups.

Wash fruit and vegetables well. Peel if required and cut into chunks.

Use fruit and vegetables in peak condition.

Prepare fruit and vegetables just before you need them. Some vitamins start to be destroyed as you cut into the produce, and some produce discolors quickly.

Add liquids such as fruit juice, milk, or yogurt to the blender first.

For maximum nutritional benefit, serve the drinks immediately after preparing them.

Smoothies may separate on standing. This does not affect the flavor. Serve with a straw twizzler or spoon to stir before drinking.

Fresh ripe fruit should provide enough natural sweetness, but you can add a little extra sugar or honey to sweeten if required.

Keep berries and chopped up soft fruit such as apricots, peaches, and bananas in the freezer to make instant iced smoothies. They can go into the blender when frozen.

Smoothies are best served cold. Chill the ingredients before use and serve with plenty of ice. Crushed ice will cool a drink quickly. You can also use ice cream or sorbet.

Smoothies tend to be thick, but you can alter the thickness of the drink to your taste. Simply add extra milk, water, or fruit juice to achieve your preferred thickness.

If the smoothie is too thin, add a banana, which is a great thickener, or some frozen ingredients such as frozen fruit or ice cream. Or use cooked rice to thicken the smoothie.

You can remove seeds, pips, or fibrous material from the smoothie by straining through a nylon sieve. This will remove the fibre content, thus affecting the nutritional value of the drink, but it is useful if you find them unpleasant or you have fussy children.

Some liquids increase in volume and froth on blending so never overfill the blender.

Make sure the lid is firmly on your blender before processing.

Wash the blender as soon as possible after use. If fruit becomes dried on, soak in warm soapy water for a few minutes to soften the fruit.

Equipment

Whether you want to make juices, smoothies, or both, there is certain equipment that will be essential to have in your kitchen.

Juices

If you want to make juice from hard fruit and vegetables such as carrots, apples, and pears, you will need to invest in a juicer. There are two main types of juicers available.

Centrifugal juicer: This is the least expensive type and it works by finely grating the fruit or vegetables and then spinning them at high speed to separate the juice from the pulp, which is then discarded.

Masticating juicer: This machine is more efficient, but it comes with a higher price tag. It finely chops the fruit, then forces the juice out through a fine mesh.

Food processor: Some types have a centrifugal juicer attachment. It will not be as efficient as a dedicated machine; however, it will be more than adequate for occasional juicing.

Citrus juicer: Citrus juicer attachments are available for some juicers and food processors. These are specifically designed to squeeze juice from citrus fruit and are the most efficient equipment for juicing this kind of fruit. However, you can squeeze citrus fruit by simply peeling and feeding the segments through the juicers. Alternatively, you may prefer to use a simple hand lemon squeezer or reamer.